GETTING THE **GREEN LIGHT** FROM GOD

Charleston, SC
www.PalmettoPublishing.com

Getting the Green Light from God

First Edition

Hardcover ISBN: 979-8-8229-0892-5
Paperback ISBN: 979-8-8229-0893-2

GETTING THE GREEN LIGHT FROM GOD

JOHN D. SHREVE

TABLE OF CONTENTS

PREFACE:

I AM A SINNER! I have done many things in my life that I regret. I am not a preacher, at least not in the professional sense. If we are Christians, we should be spreading the Gospel (Good News), especially in today's times. My Bible-reading is incomplete and I can only quote a few scriptures.

What I experienced was clearly a rare event, and I'm trying to make the most of it that I can. Also, it should quickly become obvious that I am no writer, or rather, a poor one. This attempt at writing isn't about me, or any talents I may have or not. It's about God and Jesus. When it's my time to stand before God and He asks, "Hey, I paid you a visit in 2020, what'd you do with that?" I want to have an acceptable answer.

Additionally, the events that I write about are the truth. Only the dates are fuzzy, nothing else. The rest are my opinions. Names of Mary and Sue were just made up to make a point, and I didn't mean to leave out or exclude any prophets or notable figures of the Bible.

CHAPTER ONE

THE GREEN LIGHT EVENT

It was December 26, 2020, about 1:30 a.m. I was asleep when a text came in. It was from my son Matthew who lives out of state and it simply stated, "Merry Christmas." I had left my phone on, hoping to hear from my adult children. My relationship with them has been rocky for the last few years. The text woke me up as I wasn't in a deep sleep. I opened my flip phone and read the text. I was very happy to get it! I didn't get up or turn on a light or anything. After reading the text, I closed the phone, put it back on the nightstand and said, "Thank you, GOD!" I didn't whisper it, but had someone been close by, it would've been heard.

Now, I sleep on my left side quite a bit, and I was on it when this occurred. It had only been a few minutes since the text came in and I could feel myself starting to drift. A dim green light illumination started to appear on the wall I was facing. Within a matter of seconds, the light became brighter and brighter. I was baffled! I was also now very awake. I was thinking, "What is this?" and, "What is going on?" The green light was on the outside of a large window behind me, or to my right. There were mini-blinds on the window, so the reflection of the blinds or the images of the blinds is what was appearing on the wall with a green light. The light was growing stronger and stronger.

As I lay there looking at the green illumination on the wall, I can feel my heart starting to pound. Now, I'm feeling a sense of fear. I don't know why, other than something strange and unusual is happening. I'm guessing I stared at the wall for about 15 seconds or so. I didn't get up or even move really. I didn't have to, because now the green light moved to the other window in the bedroom. This window is an up-down type and narrow. There were blinds on it and curtains, too. I kept the curtains closed with clothes pins, but about 18" from the pin to the top remained open and the blinds were visible.

It was in this exposed area, where the blinds are visible, that the green light moved to – exactly that spot. My heart started to pound even harder. I was at a loss as to what was happening and I could not believe what was happening. Other than my heart pounding (and I heard it), there was no noise. Now, to try and describe the light . . . It was ALIVE. It was not one-dimensional as one may imagine a flashlight or electric light shining. There was life and movement within the light. There was movement within it and on the edges of it. It was "alive" the entire time it was present.

Now the light was outside, yet, it somehow was visible to me inside. It was the size of about a basketball and it didn't move around or change positions. It remained at this window for about 15 to 20 seconds. It left or turned off immediately – it did not dim. Again, not a sound, only the loud thumping of my heart beating. It probably took 15 minutes or so for my heart to return to normal. At the time, I could not comprehend what I just witnessed and experienced. Surprisingly, I was able to fall back asleep within a short time. The next day, I went outside of the house to check out the windows and surrounding areas. There was nothing out of the ordinary to notice.

I shared my experience with a couple of friends soon after. One of them was a priest and good friend whom I've known for over three decades. I don't specifically remember his reaction, probably because he didn't know what to think, either. I'm sure it at least included a smile. He is always good for a smile, a chuckle, or a hearty laugh. He suggested that I share my story with his secretary, which I did, and she didn't know what to say, either. I don't recall sharing my event with anyone else until over a year later.

Now, I believe with every fiber, atom, and molecule of my being that the green light was the ALMIGHTY or a direct sign from God. My reasons are: God knows my address (Interestingly, my birthdate – month and day – are the same numbers of this address, but in a different order). Not only that, but the room in which I am sleeping. I believe it was intentional that the light appeared in the window behind me first for at least two reasons: 1) to show intelligence by moving to the other window, and; 2) to show how it manifested. The light in the first window illuminated slowly. I kind of wished that I had turned around, but I was starting to drift and was like, "Huh?"

Seeing this light appear from nothing and out of nowhere must be an awesome sight! Had I turned, though, the light may not have moved and a dimension of it may not have been witnessed. Another reason, and perhaps this should be first: Saying, "Thank you, God!" From the time I received the text until I saw the light, only a few minutes had passed. I believe what I believe. I'm still in disbelief. Disbelief that God would send me, of all people, a direct sign like this.

If the ALMIGHTY knows where I live, then He knows where I can be found sleeping. I sensed that the light appeared in the center of the first window based on how the illumination appeared on the wall. I knew this house well. I did repairs on it – plumbing, electrical, mowing and yard work, heck, I hung the blinds in the first window. The windows on this home were paper-thin and original from its construction in the '70s. Now when the light moved to the other window, it went directly to the top where no curtains were blocking.

Green. Why green? The more I had come to believe that this was indeed a Most Holy Sign, the more I couldn't help but think, "Why green?" I haven't mentioned that I'm born and raised Catholic, even Catholic-schooled all 12 years. Is "schooled" okay to use, or should I have used "educated"? Anyway, it was just a few months ago, when attending a new church (new to me), that I became aware of the same shade of green. Two long banners that went from the floor to almost the ceiling, that were hanging behind the altar, were, the exact (just about) same shade of green. After Mass, the priest was chatting with folks in the church, and when he was free, I inquired about the color green and the significance of it to the Church. He stated the green represents God and life.

A possible reason why: For about 2 years prior to my event, I'd been thinking a lot of the life of Jesus. And while living in Austin, I was encountering a number of people who weren't big on Christianity. More interested in something esoteric, like that was "cooler." Like Christianity was for the masses, and they were more enlightened. Now, that's not my thinking at all! Considering the life that Jesus led, and the miracles he performed, how could any kind of guru compare? Even His first miracle of turning water into wine at a wedding party. Let's try to imagine that scenario: Mary (Our Holy Mother) coming up to Jesus and saying, "Son, I'm going to need you to do me a favor." Now, imagine the humanity here, a mother and son. The depth of love a mother feels for her child, and, knowing WHO your son really is. As we know, Jesus did her that favor, and only for Her. He loved His Mother, and I believe he really loved all His disciples and their relations. His prayers in the garden before being turned over – He knew what was on the other side of the upcoming Paradise with God, but to me, Jesus had grown to love these people, humans. He was going to miss them!

I guess the repeated encounters with people who were atheists, or something other than Christians, made me think about and appreciate Jesus all the more. God sending His only Son to us, for our sake, makes a lot of sense to me, too. I can appreciate this gift from God even more as a parent.

Here's another reason: The light never entered the house. And why would it? Since it was Holy, it wouldn't, being that the house wasn't sanctified. Now for clarification, the light seemed to have appeared through the blinds. I can't explain how, only that I could still see it, all of it, despite the fact that the blinds were there and should have blocked the light. It's as if the blinds disappeared to allow me to see it, and I can believe that happened.

I will explain other events that took place IN the house that were of a dark/evil nature, but not at this time.

Another reason: Timing. I get a text, I thank God, and the next event is the appearance of the light. All of this in about 300 seconds or less in the middle of the night.

Here are some end-of-chapter clarifications and fill-ins: The date of December 26 is for certain. The time is approximate. As for the year of 2020, I'm pretty sure. The location of the 2nd window was to the left of the bed and me. Since I was already lying on my left side, I didn't have to move to view the Green-Light (ball). I don't think I moved at all.

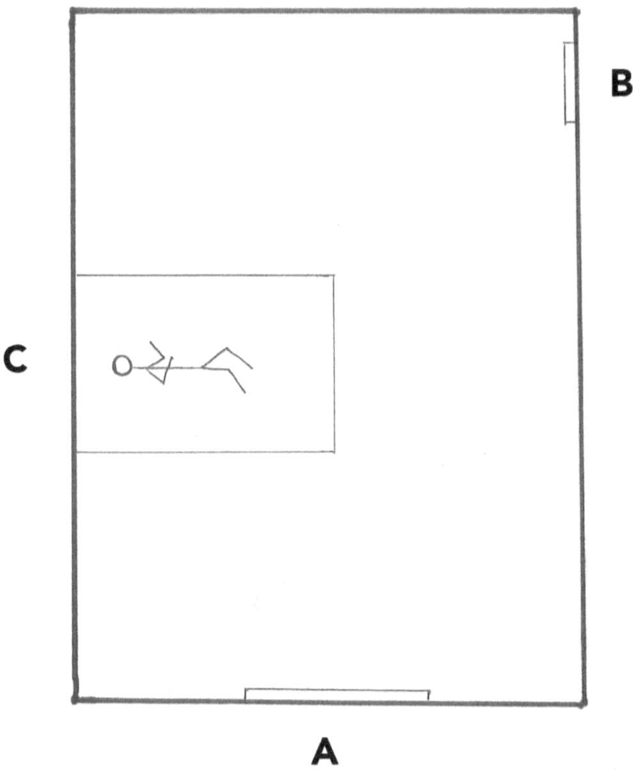

A = initial location of the green light manifestation that I did not observe directly

B = second location of the green light that I observed directly

C = location of my bed where I was laying

CHAPTER TWO

NOT-SO-NICE STUFF

AND NOW FOR SOMETHING

completely different. The unclean. As I was laying in bed this morning thinking about the next chapter to write, I realized that the order of events wasn't immediately clear to me. I didn't document anything. I got to thinking that the order of events may be telling.

Let's start with the flying black ball. One sunny afternoon (same address/house), while sitting in an easy chair, in the living room watching TV, a small black ball, a little bigger than a golf ball, approximately, came floating/flying out of the hallway. It was about 3 feet up from the floor. As soon as I turned my head to the right to view it, it made an almost per-fect 360-degree circle downward, proceeding a little more to my right, and then flew in front of me at eye level and about two feet away. It then went to the bottom of the patio door window, through it, and disappeared once it hit the window. Also, it made a noise as it hit the glass, similar to an insect hitting a window. This all took place in a matter of seconds, maybe four or five. It did not appear to be solid. It seemed mist-like and while "black" seems best to describe the col-or, maybe there was something dark gray to it. Other than the window exit, it made no noise. I sensed intelligence to it since it flew right in front of me, and by the downward loop at the moment I noticed it. To me, the downward movement signified evil.

Here's another: One sunny and bright Texas morning as I'm sleeping, I am awakened by a noise. I kept by bedroom door ajar because of my cat, Riggs. The noise was coming from a spot in the kitchen only about six or seven feet away. I have never heard a noise like it, before or since. It sounded somewhat human-like with an intention to be annoying and irritating. Also, I detected different frequencies and fluctuations in tone and volume. The duration of the event was about 10 seconds or less. I, of course, woke up and looked through the crack of the open door in the direction the noise and saw nothing. I got up and stayed up looking about . . . nothing.

I believe that these two incidents happened before my green light experience, however, I am not sure.

I've seen, I've heard, and now on to the touching. As I stated previously, about the sequence and order of events, was there an order for a reason? Let me be very clear here. I'm not claiming to be an expert on anything. I 'm telling and writing about events that happened to me. I believe in God and His Son, Jesus! The Bible clearly points out the existence of Satan and unclean spirits, so, through God's Divine Plan, these things exist. To me, the existence of ghosts is extremely rare and is only allowed with God's permission, as written in the Bible. It's SIMPLE: It's either from God, or from Satan! My Green Light was from God! ALL the other occurrences were evil!

The touching: The three incidents involving the touching of my feet occurred over several months. Exact dates/times I don't know and I didn't write anything down. I'm asleep, in the middle of the night, I feel a tip of a finger quickly flick or slide up on the bottom of my foot (arch). For the record, I'm usually a light sleeper. I was awakened by this touch immediately. I jerked my leg in reaction. I was startled and didn't know what to think. I fell back asleep and nothing else happened that night.

This happened again a few months later. Pretty much the same thing: asleep, finger, wake up. This time, though, I'm taking action. Next day, I'm off to the store for a St. Michael candle!

Every night since the second touch, I prayed to St. Michael and lit the candle. As I stated, I'm a light sleeper and sometimes the flickering of the candle on the ceiling would bother my sleep. I always kept the candle on a chest of drawers just opposite of my bed, and this was close to where my feet were. Well, one night I moved the candle farther away to a small dresser off to the side of my bed. I did this because the flickering was keeping me awake. A few hours pass and I'm in a deep sleep when on my left foot, I feel major fingertips scratching almost like done to tickle. This isn't a quick fingertip flick. It's repeated up and down on the step area, just below the toes. I awake and it stops. This was startling! I immediately got up and moved the St. Michael candle back to the original spot. I went back to bed, finally fell asleep, and nothing else happened.

During the time of all my events, I'd been listening to radio shows at night as I would fall asleep. The shows dealt in the weird areas of life – the paranormal, UFOs, science, etc. Once the touching incidents started, I veered away from the darker topics of the shows. I am no longer in this house. I've since moved out of Austin. Still in Texas, but in another house. While still in the process of moving into the new place, I contacted a local Catholic church to set up a house-blessing.

When I called the church, the secretary took down my info and request. She called me back a few days later, telling me that Deacon So & So would be coming to do the Blessing. The Deacon's name didn't even register because as soon as I heard "deacon," I politely informed her that I needed a "priest"! She seemed annoyed at my demand but I didn't share with her my recent experiences. A few days later, one of the priests from the church came in and did a great and very thorough Blessing.

Kind of in line with blessings, I think I learned something. When praying, especially for protection, don't yell or even raise your voice. Raising your voice is sending a signal of acknowledgement, and you DON'T want to do that. NEVER communicate! Not with something dark. Only to Jesus, Mary, an Angel, or God. Also, the Power is in the words of the prayer and rest assured, that's all you need. Believe in the words and in the prayer!

The occult, or close enough. At the time of the flying black ball and the freaky noise in the kitchen, I was watching a lot of "ghost" shows. I'd always been interested in the paranormal. I have come now to believe that these shows can be dangerous, especially those with "actual" recordings of voices, howls, and other unknown noises. Now, I believe unclean and evil spirits are very much prowling about, looking for those interested in death and answers to the unknown. I am no longer curious because I now know what I need to know. Evil is very real and can come in many forms. Good is from God and there is NOTHING in the middle!

So, my advice to you is to stay away from psychics, tarot cards, paranormal shows, etc. If you want answers, you won't find any there. Satan is the Master of Lies and will only lead you astray.

It's written somewhere, ". . . better to rule in Hell than to serve in Heaven." YOU think you're going to rule in Hell? Satan is just going to say to you, "Yeah, you take over for a while. I need a break. I've been doing this long enough." If you find yourself in Hell, you won't be ruling anything, no matter how bad you were on Earth. And what about UFOs and Bigfoot? Well, I saw a UFO. It was a flying black ball in my living room. Where did it come from? Where was it going? Why did it disappear when it hit the window? Was it flying invisibly outside in the daylight? Was it interdimensional? Clearly, Satan has powers, and if he has powers, he will use them. Hey, why not use your powers to distract, ask questions, cause doubt, confuse, etc.?

Reincarnation. Good ol' reincarnation. Hmmm, let's see, how does that work? Okay, so you just died. Now what? So, your spirit or your soul starts flying around, thinking, "Maybe?" Unless you already know what or who you want to be reincarnated into? Let's say you want to be a horse

– just an example. I guess you have to fly around looking for a pregnant horse. What if another soul or spirit wants the same and is waiting there, too? What if this other soul got there first? Any rules on how this works? If so, who wrote the rules? Who enforces them?

Throughout our history, haven't there been many who were curious about reincarnation? Didn't some say that if it were real, they'd come back and tell us? Also, doesn't this present a mathematical problem? If souls are being recycled, then won't we need more new ones . . . population increase. Where do the new ones come from?

Reincarnation is rubbish. There have been some documentations of people coming up with some strange memories, etc. I believe these to be nothing more than evil tricks to distract or cause doubts. I realize that it can be disturbing and unsettling to accept the fact that Satan and evil spirits are really prowling the Earth looking for those who are full of pride, those who are hurting, those looking for acceptance, those who are scared and those who don't know what to believe in. The list is endless. All you have to do is look around. Satan is very much alive and doing quite well, by his standards.

At the time of the green light incident, I hadn't been going to Mass. I'd go to church to pray and light candles, if they had them, but attending an actual Mass was rare. I want to say the evil seeing and hearing incidents happened before the green light, but I'm not really sure. I do know that the touching incidents occurred after the green light visit. One reason is because my bedroom was completely dark when it happened. The St. Michael candles would've interfered with the scenario. Also, I made a realization just today that I over-looked earlier: I wear corrective lenses! Glasses and contacts. The green light night, I saw it ALL without ANY glasses on! I don't wear contacts to bed, and I don't need my glasses to read. I didn't put them on to read my son's text. I can't be-lieve that that didn't occur to me until today!

To clarify about the black ball: I KNOW bugs and insects! Here in Texas, we've got them. I have caught a hundred wasps in the house in an empty tennis ball can and released them outside. Big water-roaches can fly, but they are noisy when they do. It is rare and highly unlikely for them to do a 360-degree movement, even a sloppy one. Beetles, lizards, you name it, I've caught or handled a ton. The black ball was not of this world or dimension.

CHAPTER THREE

GOD, JESUS, AND THE WORLD

WHAT OR WHO IS GOD? WELL, here are my thoughts. God is beyond human comprehension. I've heard numerous times from people that they don't want God to be this bearded old guy in a robe. How one-dimensional is that? Let's take the size of the Earth. Does the word "massive" describe it? No, I don't think so. The oceans are massive. We've got the planets: the sun, moon, Mars, and the Earth. I picture God keeping the sun aflame with one of His nostrils, spinning the Earth with His pinky finger, keeping every heart beating (that should be), sending green light-balls to people saying, "Thank you," and making sure everything is in motion as He set it to be.

For thousands of years, man has been looking to the sky and sun, making sacrifices of plants, animals, and even humans, thanking whatever is up there for the sun, rain, crops, etc. God knows of every sacrifice made. Then God sent His sacrifice to us, Jesus. He had the Prophets write about it and a Covenant was made. Jesus then came to Earth to join the fun. He walked, talked, and did things that *no one* could've done. CRUCIFIED and came back to show His Apostles, and send them on their way with absolute proof. Would you die for a lie? I wouldn't and neither would the Apostles. But they all died for the truth (except one) and suffered horrible deaths defending the words and actions of Jesus.

From what we understand, God created Heaven (a party, let's say) and the angels. All was going well until one of the angels, Lucifer, grew envious of God. Lucifer and a third of the angels were kicked out of Heaven. Lucifer was sent to Earth. God wants a new party, BUT can't just invite *anybody* to the new party. God needs to *know* the *heart* of everyone first! God doesn't want another Lucifer-repeat! So, have you ever thrown a party and invited *everyone* you knew? Maybe that didn't go well either – lesson learned? Next party, *some* may not be invited, and some *for sure* will. Could life on Earth, God, Heaven, Jesus be summed up with invitations and a grand party?

There's a lot to the Bible that has me with . . . questions. Especially the Old Testament. God seemed to be right there for Adam and Eve, Cain and Abel, and Noah. Did He just speak and never materialize? Why would Cain speak to God in a snappy and disrespectful tone, knowing he was speaking to God? Also, there is some plurality used with "Our" instead of "My." The Old Testament is filled with wars and God "backing" the good guys. God is angry a lot in the Old Testament, and understandably so, even with all His miracles and signs during the Exodus, angel visitations, etc. Did God make adjustments to "Man" after the Flood? Men were living up to the age of almost a thousand years. I can't say I know much, but I know enough and I know the most important part of it all: God is real and so is Jesus! Some say they are one and the same. I don't know, but I don't think so. I hope to one day give Jesus a big hug and a kiss on the cheek, and thank Him for His sacrifice on the Cross. To COMPLETELY humble Himself for my sake and for humanity.

If you've never touched a Bible, or opened one. If you're unfamiliar with the life of Jesus, it's not too late. According to one of His parables, it's never too late. (You have to be alive, though.)

With all that's been going on in our country and the world, a lot of people have lost their way. People don't know what to believe in, where to turn, or what to do. Now is a bad time to not be grounded in something. Give God and Jesus a chance! There are no contracts to sign. You can approach God at your comfort level. Since I'm Catholic, of course I'll send you in the direction of a Catholic Church, but any Christian church will do. I have always sensed peace when I walk into an empty church.

If you're lucky enough to live near an old church., sometimes the windows and/or the architecture can be inspiring. Go in, sit down, clear your mind. Talk to God. Of course, I can't guarantee a visual response, but I can guarantee HE is listening. I knew someone who thought of God as their personal genie, but God is no one's genie. God is God, the only One to place every star in the sky. And, at the same time, WANTS to hear from us. Each and every one of us. I wrote in the Preface that I'm not a preacher, but I'm starting to sound like one. What can I do, though, since I get a marvelous sign just for thanking Him? I think I'm doing what I'm supposed to do, sharing my experience and how it relates to my beliefs. Most importantly, so that YOU may come to believe, too!

God the Creator. God is an artist. What do artists do? They keep stuff they created that they like, and throw away the stuff they don't like. Artists experiment. One may paint and then try to sculpt. So, clearly God created dinosaurs sometime well before man. Why? To experiment with His creativity? All creatures before us are no longer here, but we are! Jesus came to save Humanity, not dinosaurs. We are all that matter to God now, and NOW is what matters.

As for dinosaurs, or "fossil fuels," I don't believe it. We've been drilling for oil and crude for over a century now, and the supply seems endless. "Fossils," or the supply of, would've or should've run out by now. Everything has its limits. There are only so many trees in a forest, only so much water in a lake. According to scientists, the Earth was mostly water. How could millions or billions of dinosaurs have existed on a small land mass, with limited resources and food supply? Also, shouldn't dinosaurs throw a monkey-wrench into the theory of evolution? Some creatures were huge, some were not. Which is it? Which way are things evolving – bigger or smaller? A lot of our established theories are just that – "theories." Obviously, I don't know what "crude" is, but I don't believe the established theory.

There's a recording out there, supposedly taken in the Earth's deepest hole (Siberia). Scientists dropped a microphone as far as they could and captured what basically sounds like "Hell." They captured wailing, moans, and what one would consider the expected sounds of souls being tortured. It was stated that the scientists grabbed their gear and go the "hell" out of there. True? Who knows? And what about the sun? What are the theories there? How can we *truly* know? We can't! Shouldn't it have burned up by now? What is its fuel source? According to our theories, everything needs a fuel source, right? Dead dinosaurs equal crude. The sun is floating in our galaxy at a perfect distance with a consistent temperature. God is the source for the sun, like He is the source for your beating heart. Why is your heart beating? What brand of batteries are in your chest? It's been said that the more we discover, the less we know, or something like that, scientifically speaking, of course. There are those who will live and die by science, no God! As I stated earlier with the word "massive," what word or words can define our universe? None!

So, maybe some scientific theories are wrong. I'm thinking that "dating" things chronologically is not quite accurate. Once we go further into time, we're just guessing. Going back millions of years seems impractical. I'm thinking that about 10,000 years or so is about the best we can do. God can spin the Earth, or the planets, or the galaxy at any rate He chooses. Maybe the Earth was mostly land and not water so our future "fossil fuels" could thrive and make our crude. If our crude is from prehistoric creatures, then good thing God made so many of them, and good for God, too! Since the discovery and use of crude and oil-derivatives, the Earth's population boomed for about 1 billion to 8 billion. Is that a bad thing? NO! You and I would probably not be around had this not occurred! Billions more for God and Jesus to welcome into Heaven. All the more to know of Jesus and to benefit from His sacrifice.

CHAPTER FOUR

MARY, SUE, AND A LADY

THE STORY OF MARY AND

Sue. Mary owns a business and is mega-wealthy. Her employees don't know that she is the owner as she passes herself off as just another employee. Along comes Sue, a single mom living in a small apartment. Sue is friendly and likes to talk. Some time passes and Mary grows quite fond of Sue and her kids. Mary decides to rig up a fake raffle so that she can provide Sue with a brand-new home.

Sue moves into her new home and within a short time is ready to throw a house-warming party. Mary is very talented and creative. She enjoys painting, sculpting, etc. She decides to make the perfect vase. It will match the color scheme of Sue's house and will even be inlaid with precious jewels. The time has come for the party and the house is packed with Sue's former neighbors, her new ones, friends, relatives, etc. Now Mary arrives with her handmade vase tucked in a gift bag. Sue lets Mary in, gives her a one-arm hug, and introduces Mary to a few people close by. Mary tells her that she made a beautiful vase just for her and her home. Sue peeks in the bag as she walks Mary to a chair tucked in the corner of the room. Sue comments that it is very nice. Mary is seated and within a matter of seconds, Sue is called over to admire a different gift from someone else. Some time passes and a few guests visit with Mary and acknowledge the beautiful vase and how perfectly it matches the décor. Throughout the party, Mary is mostly ignored along with her gift. Sue is having a great time enjoying the food, wine, and her other guests.

As the party winds down, Sue walks Mary to the door and thanks her for coming, and for the nice gift.

Things are back to normal at work, when somehow Sue is informed that Mary gifted her the house. So, on her lunch break, Sue stops at a store and buys a "Thank You" card. She signs her name to it and upon her return to work, she sets it on Mary's desk. The end.

Now, stop. Stop and really think about this fictional story and Mary If you were Mary, how would you feel? To you, these just might be words on paper, but are they? In the story, Mary and Sue are both people. Is the true meaning of the story coming through? In reality, Mary represents God. Mary's perfect gift is Jesus. Sue represents US, too many of us. Let's add another dimension to this. In the story, Mary is a person. In reality, though, we're talking about God. Do you have God sitting in the corner while you ignore Him and His Gift? Is your thanks and appreciation for all of God' Gifts sealed in a quick "Thank You" card?

Again, I ask you, how would you feel? Everything we can do and have: walk, talk, run, smile, eat, play, as well as your food, house, car, children, pets, friends, everything, is a Gift! Is your expression of appreciation even less than a "Thank You" card? Is it better or easier for you not to even believe in God?

I recently met a lady, and shortly thereafter we went for a bite to eat. We chatted, of course, and got along just fine. I asked her about her religion, and she stated that she was raised in a Protestant denomination. Also, that as soon as she was able, she got out of it because of the hypocrisy she witnessed there. As for her current view of religion, she shared that she believed in something, a Creator. She believed in reincarnation and in being a good person. There was more, but all on the same track.

This lady is retired, had a good career (a professional), and in my experience, shares a common view with a lot of people in this same age range and demographic. Which is sad. No mention of Jesus. Jesus came to fill the loop-holes, to dot the i's and cross the t's, and to complete what His Father started. With the work and Word of Jesus, we can't wiggle out of our responsibility. That's a good thing, though, accepting our faults is the first step towards our freedom. To acknowledge our weaknesses, we have to humble ourselves and not to think that we are awesome. God is awesome, and Jesus was and is awesome. The Garden of Eden, Adam and Eve. The serpent lied to Eve, telling her that eating the forbidden fruit would make them like God. No, no matter what, we can't even come close! Space travel, medical advances, whatever – we will have our limits. And the best we will ever do still won't even come close.

So, as you read this, you may find yourself in a bad spot in life. Maybe you're addicted to drugs, sex, alcohol, or something worse. Or, maybe you're in a position where you think you've got it made. Done with school, a great career, a nice house, lots of friends, etc. You're living for you. Very common. I've lived for me, too! The here and now is great! What about there and later? You won't always be young. You can't take it with you! Is this all there is? As we understand it, the rich man in the Bible who ignored Lazarus (the poor one), wasn't condemned because of his wealth, rather it was because of his greed and ignorance of those less fortunate. God searches the Heart. The heart of the rich man was obvious – cold.

Whatever spot you find yourself in, it's not too late! Jesus and God are there. God is listening, as He is everywhere. Never, ever did I expect the Green Light!

CHAPTER FIVE

SAVE THE PLANET TIPS, ETC.

I'M GUESSING THAT THIS IS the only book I'll ever write, so I may as well speak my mind about everything. Maybe it all relates. As I write, I should point out the date: It's November, 2022. Over the past few years everyone knows what's been going on in the world: Covid, major political issues, inflation, war with Russia and Ukraine, and now talk of China invading Taiwan. All this going on in the world and the Almighty is saying, "Hey," or "You're welcome," to some guy in Texas who was happy to hear from his son.

It's easy to blame God for all the crap that we create. Or, to wonder why He would let all these bad things go on. But if we blame or ask why, we're not looking at the big picture. We'd have to ask God to take away our free will. It's our free will that allows us to make poor decisions, or evil ones, or selfish ones.

Also, we need to stop taking the Lord's name in vain! When someone says, "Oh, my God!" they're taking the Lord's name in vain. Do NOT call or mention "God" unless you mean it! That's why someone invented "gosh." And while we're at it, it's "I couldn't care less," not "I could care less." Too many people are saying this wrong. Back to the name of God. Take it from me, He *is* listening.

JOHN D. SHREVE

MY CONTRIBUTIONS TO HELP SAVE THE PLANET:

I'm still not seeing ANY attempts to synchronize stoplights!? Why not? Doing this would help the planet in two ways: First, the less time vehicles are sitting and waiting for red lights, the less exhaust emissions. Second, it'll save on fuel consumption. Doing this only requires effort and man-hours/ equipment. Light synchronization should be started immediately. There is NO good reason not to.

Traffic studies should be started immediately for right-turn lane improvements. The same reasons, effort, and benefits apply as with light synchronization. Again, NO reason not to! Funding can be raised with a Drive-thru Tax for fast food restaurants. Personally, I prefer to dine in or go in to a restaurant instead of wasting gas and emitting more gas fumes.

An inexpensive air purifier machine can be found at any major department store. The machine functions quite simply. A fan moves air in one direction and we have airflow. Airflow creates suction on one end and forces or blows air out of the other end. A filter collects particles (dust, dander, etc.) flowing through the air since it is positioned between the flow. Simple concept. Industrial versions should be placed on top of buildings to collect pollution, emissions, gasses, etc. They can be solar-powered. Metal, filters, and solar cells, that's it. Man-power and effort to install. What reasons are there NOT to do this? Isn't something better than nothing, especially if the planet is in a state of emergency, as being claimed?

And what about hemp? It is my understanding that before we started ripping through our forests for paper, that hemp was used as paper, and it had other uses, to, such as rope, clothing, etc. I'm not hearing about hemp in the works to help save our planet! Again, another simple step. Maybe it's in the works, but I haven't heard anything. Don't trees act as a natural filter for the environment, and help clean our air? I recently went to my local home improvement store for some lumber. When I got it home, I noticed a tag on it that read "Made in Sweden." That's a long way from the U.S.! How did it get here? On an ocean freighter using fuel. As a homeowner, I've been to the home improvement stores for several items. Lighting fixtures . . . NOT made in our country! Too high-tech, maybe? Tools . . . NOT made in our country.

My previous vehicle was older with a lot of miles on it, so that meant repairs and parts replacements. Off to the auto parts stores. Parts made here? Nope! Not even brake rotors! More ocean freighters using fuel and spewing emissions all across our oceans. If we produced our own good here, goods that we need and will use, wouldn't that cut out the use of fuel of transport and the emissions of? Wouldn't that help save our planet? I heard a long time ago that there was a floating pollution-pile the size of Texas in one of our oceans. If true, it must be the size of Alaska by now.

Here's another "Save the Planet" tip: Down here in the part of Texas, people like to go "tubing." On a hot day, folks get into big inner tubes, drink beer, and float on a cool river. The problem? Well, a lot of these tubers come to the river *slathered* in sunscreen. Most sunscreens are full of chemicals, and the longer one stays in the water, the more will wash off. So, the fish, frogs, fowl, and turtles get their natural habitat polluted with chemicals. Simple fix? Don't wear sunscreen, maybe? Now, I've never heard this issue every brought up at any time, but I think something should be done. Our natural water supply is important and limited, especially in the drought conditions we are experiencing.

I am no genius, but even these simple ideas can help the environment. High-tech solutions aren't always required. I'm not hearing *any* simple suggestions! Occasionally, I'll see a news report about a child or teenager setting up a recycling program or event, but that's all I'm hearing. Low-tech solutions can help, especially if applied on a broad scale. Green energy is a step in the right direction; however, it is not the solution, at least not now. For example, everything needed to make an electric car requires resources from hard-to-dig minerals (usually in third-world countries and labored by children), and oil-derived products (plastics, etc.) to make the actual vehicle.

As I write all this, it's just weeks away from the year 2023. 2023! We have computers to wear as watches, and we have weekly flights to space. And, we have third-world countries! Why? We've advanced and accomplished so much, yet we still have people living in these countries digging through piles of garbage looking for food and/or clothes. How many countries have yet to set up clean water and sewer systems? Why? Why in the year of 2023 is this still a problem anywhere? There's a war going on in Ukraine, and those citizens have had their lives ruined, disrupted, etc. War is a terrible thing, and attention and resources are being sent as should be done. We can assume, though, that this will come to an end. Where are the world organizations speaking out against continuing third-world issues?

Why is it okay for children to be worked in these countries and barely a peep? Since the start of the Ukraine/Russia war I've seen a thousand news segments on TV, but not one about 8-, 9-, and 10-year-olds going without clean drinking water, or working 12-hour days for a dollar! Why is this? We've been building dams, sewers, factories for centuries. We can't do, show, help or provide assistance to get these countries to join us in the modern age?

Now for the best save the planet (and humans) tip: STAY MARRIED! Divorced parents are running two households with all the double everything: refrigerators, other appliances and needed utilities, etc. All the gas/fuel driving and exchanging the kids for visitations. Recently, I met a couple of gentlemen on the tennis court. One has been married over 40 years, and the other over 60 years (yes, he's in his 80s and still plays tennis. It's a great sport.) I couldn't make it to even 10 years, but my brain/smarts didn't kick in until around the age of 35. Two couples with over a century of marriage -- that's dedication, commitment, and quite an achievement!

On a side-note – something for already divorced parents to consider: What is greater? The love for your children or the contempt for your Ex? Whichever, the greater will eventually manifest! Please, don't ever use your children as tools for revenge! God did not create them for that! If you do this, the results will be disastrous and, in time, YOU will see and live with those results, whether it be drug abuse, alcoholism, countless meaningless relationships, or worse. DO what is best for your children, NOT what ticks off your Ex! So, ask yourself: Which is greater? Love for my kids? Or hate for my Ex? Time and life will provide the TRUE answer.

You WILL serve,
whether it be Man or God . . .

Man is weak.
Man is corruptible.

God is pure. God is love.
God is just.

God is here, there and always.
Choose God.

www.ingramcontent.com/pod-product-compliance
Lightning Source LLC
Chambersburg PA
CBHW031002180726
47993CB00018B/1517